Sport in the UK

Edited by Christina Hughes

Series Editor: Cara Acred

Vol. 96

Independence Educational Publishers

First published by Independence

The Studio, High Green, Great Shelford

Cambridge CB22 5EG

England

© Independence 2015

British Library Cataloguing in Publication Data

Sport in the UK. -- (Issues today ; 96)

1. Sports--Social aspects--Great Britain--Juvenile literature. 2. Sports--Moral and ethical aspects--Great Britain--Juvenile literature.

I. Series II. Acred, Cara editor.

306.4'83'0941-dc23

ISBN-13: 9781861686992

Acknowledgements

The publisher is grateful for permission to reproduce the material in this book. While every care has been taken to trace and acknowledge copyright, the publisher tenders its apology for any accidental infringement or where copyright has proved untraceable. The publisher would be pleased to come to a suitable arrangement in any such case with the rightful owner.

Illustrations

All illustrations, including the front cover, are by Don Hatcher.

Images

Pages 1, 6: © Jackie Staines, page 7: MorgueFile, page 9: MorgueFile, page 22: iStock, page 23: iStock, page 26: icons by Freepik.

Editorial by Christina Hughes and layout by Jackie Staines, on behalf of Independence Educational Publishers.

Printed in Great Britain by Zenith Print Group.

Cara Acred

Cambridge

January 2015

Contents

About *ISSUES* today

ISSUES **today** is a series of resource books on contemporary social issues, designed for Key Stage 3 pupils and above. This series is also suitable for Scottish P7, S1 and S2 students.

Each volume contains information from a variety of sources, including government reports and statistics, newspaper and magazine articles, surveys and polls, academic research and literature from charities and lobby groups. The information has been tailored to an 11 to 14 age group; it has been rewritten and presented in a simple, straightforward and accessible format.

In addition, each *ISSUES* **today** title features handy tasks and assignments based on the information contained in the book, for use in class, for homework or as a revision aid.

ISSUES **today** can be used as a learning resource in a variety of Key Stage 3 subjects, including English, Science, History, Geography, PSHE, Citizenship, Sex and Relationships Education and Religious Education.

About this book

Sport in the UK is Volume 96 in the *ISSUES* **today** series.

The role of sport in our society is constantly changing. This book considers sport's function within society and looks at controversies surrounding the topic, such as doping and racism. It also explores issues of gender, disability and religion in sport.

Sport in the UK offers a useful overview of the many issues involved in this topic. However, at the end of each article is a URL for the relevant organisation's website, which can be visited by pupils who want to carry out further research.

Because the information in this book is gathered from a number of different sources, pupils should think about the origin of the text and critically evaluate the information that is presented. Does the source have a particular bias or agenda? Are you being presented with facts or opinions? Do you agree with the writer?

At the end of each chapter there are two pages of activities relating to the articles and issues raised in that chapter. The 'Brainstorm' questions can be done as a group or individually after reading the articles. This should prompt some ideas and lead on to further activities. Some suggestions for such activities are given under the headings 'Oral', 'Moral dilemmas', 'Research', 'Written' and 'Design' that follow the 'Brainstorm' questions.

For more information about *ISSUES* **today** and its sister series, *ISSUES* (for pupils aged 14 to 18), please visit the Independence website.

Sport and society

Sport and young people

A 2014 Sport England review into young people's lives found that sport needs to adapt how it presents itself. This will help to increase the amount of young people who play sport regularly:

➤ Young people's behaviours do not always reflect their attitudes to sport – we need to focus more on changing behaviours instead of attitudes.

➤ Many young people take part in sport/activity for more functional or lifestyle reasons – keep engaging them and providing feedback on what actually matters to them not what matters to sport.

➤ Sport can provoke strong emotional responses. Whilst the activity can be sport, the message that sells it doesn't have to be. Levelling the playing field can also help overcome the emotional baggage of sport.

➤ Sport often has to compete or connect with wider interests or priorities. Young people respond well to meaningful experiences; those which benefit them as an individual, reinforce their place in their social group or help them develop.

➤ The supply of sport tends to reach those already engaged. Young people, particularly those in their late teens/early 20s, need to feel the community sport offer is specific enough to their needs and fits with their lives.

Sport and older people

The sporting habit declines with age, but people are often keen to go on exercising with the right support.

Research among recently retired people suggests that the social component, fun and enjoyment of exercise are important motivators.

Its recommendations include:

➤ positive messages, including reassurances about safety

➤ taster sessions

➤ avoid the word 'sport'

➤ make opportunities as local as possible

➤ promote the opportunities available to this age group.

Sport and sexual orientation

Sport take-up is high among gay men and lesbian women, according to the latest Active People survey.

Lesbian and bisexual women are more likely to take part in sport than all women – 44% play sport at least once a week, compared to just over 30% of all women according to analysis of Active People Survey data in 2012 (APS 6 Q2 results).

Gay men are also more likely than the overall male population to take part in sport, though participation is not as high for bisexual men.

The data also reveals that sexual orientation influences the type of sport people take up. Gay and bisexual males are less likely to take part in team sports, while lesbian and bisexual females are more likely to do so.

Sport and ethnicity

The number of people playing sport varies widely by ethnic group.

Analysis carried out in 2012 on Active People Survey data (APS 6 Q2 results) showed take-up is higher among people from mixed background, with 44% playing sport at least once a week.

Among other ethnic groups, participation varies very little for men. Among women, however, females from white backgrounds are also more likely to take part in sport compared to people from Chinese, other and black backgrounds, with a low of 21% for females from Asian backgrounds.

Across sport as a whole, 89% of those who take part are from white and 11% from non-white backgrounds (88% of the English population are from white backgrounds). But this varies in specific sports.

In basketball and cricket, for instance, over a third are from non-white backgrounds; badminton and football also have a higher than average proportion of players from these groups. On the other hand, non-white players make up a small share of cyclists and golfers.

Sport and faith groups

Faith has an influence on sports take-up, especially among some groups of women.

People who state they have no religion are more likely to take part in sport.

Analysis carried out in 2012 on Active People Survey data (APS 6 Q2 results) showed participation is also high among Sikh, Muslim and Buddhist men. But it is much lower for women of the same faiths, compared with the overall female population.

There are also notable differences among different sports. For instance, badminton, basketball and cricket all have higher take-up rates for Buddhist, Hindu, Jewish, Sikh and Muslim faiths as compared with those stating a Christian faith or no religion. In football, however, this rate is the same as for people who say they have no religion.

Sport and the economy

Hard economic times have had a big impact on the take-up of sport.

A study commissioned by Sport England found that one of the side-effects of recession is that less people are taking part in sport.

Past evidence from the 1980s and 1990s suggests that economic recessions did not have a major effect on sports participation. However, the latest paper found clear evidence that the recession which began in 2008 has had a 'significant negative effect'.

The effect was more obvious in expensive sports such as sailing, skiing and golf. Sports such as running continued to grow.

The above information is reprinted with kind permission from Sport England.
© Sport England 2014

www.sportengland.org

Mini glossary

Participation – *to take part in, to be involved with.*

Inclusive – *including/to include.*

Recession – *a temporary period of decline in economic activity (there is a widespread drop in the spending of money).*

Who plays sport?

The national picture.

Sport England's data gives an insight into who plays sport and how they play it.

Sport England's data for 2013/14 shows that:

➤ 15.6 million adults now play sport at least once a week. That's 1.7 million more than in 2005/6.
➤ Over 900,000 14–15-year-olds play sport at least once a week.
➤ Most adults – 52% – still do not play sport.
➤ 17.4% of adults now take part in at least three sport sessions a week – up from 15.5% in 2005/6.

Who plays sport?

The number of adults who play sport at least once a week is on the rise – but just over half of all adults play no sport.

There are a number of key factors in sports participation:

Gender

Gender has a big influence on sports take-up. More men play sport than women. Currently 40.9% of men play sport at least once a week, compared to 30.3% of women. At a younger age, men are much more likely than women to play sport. But this difference declines sharply with age.

Age and socio-economic groups

Age is a factor in participation: 54.5% of 16- to 25-year-olds (58.0% of 14–25-year-olds) take part in at least one sport session a week, compared to 32.0% of older adults (age 26-plus).

Take-up is highest among managerial/professional workers and intermediate social groups. It is lowest among manual workers and unemployed people.

Ethnicity and disability

The number of both black and minority ethnic and white British adults playing sport is increasing. More disabled

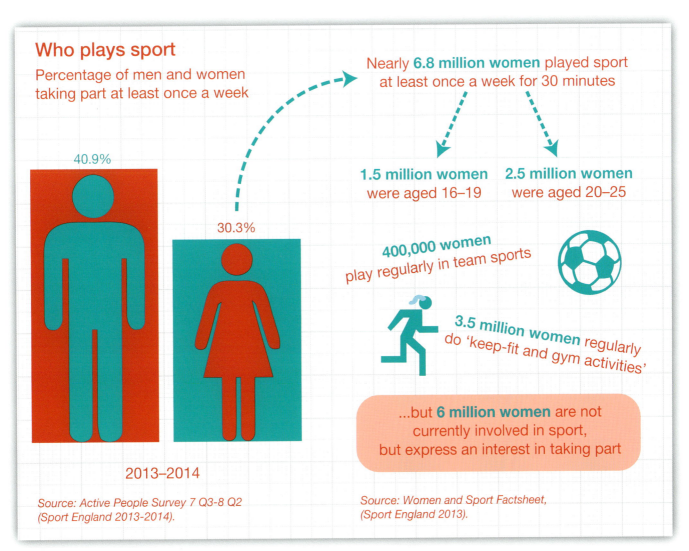

Who plays sport

Percentage of men and women taking part at least once a week

40.9%

30.3%

2013–2014

Source: Active People Survey 7 Q3-8 Q2 (Sport England 2013-2014).

Nearly **6.8 million women** played sport at least once a week for 30 minutes

1.5 million women were aged 16–19

2.5 million women were aged 20–25

400,000 women play regularly in team sports

3.5 million women regularly do 'keep-fit and gym activities'

...but **6 million women** are not currently involved in sport, but express an interest in taking part

Source: Women and Sport Factsheet, (Sport England 2013).

people are taking part in sport – latest results show 17.8% are playing sport regularly, up from 15.1% in 2005/6.

How do people take part?

As well as playing sport, the Active People Survey data shows how people are involved in sport – for instance, through club membership, tuition or coaching, through competitive sport or as volunteers.

➤ Over 9.2 million people (16-plus) are members of a sports club – 21% of the English population.

➤ Around 7.3 million people (16-plus) received sports coaching in 2013/14, while 5.7 million took part in competitive sport. Both activities have declined since 2005/6.

➤ There are also over 2.9 million people (16-plus) who volunteer regularly in sport, according to the latest figures.

By sport

Examine the popularity of different sports and how people engage with them – whether through organised competitions, club membership or tuition.

Who plays sport?

Swimming, athletics, cycling and football are amongst the most popular sports in 2013/14:

➤ Over 2.9 million people were swimming once a week in 2013/14, making it the top sport by a significant margin.

➤ The number of people taking part in athletics weekly has risen from 1.4 million in 2005/6 to over 2.1 million today.

➤ The number of weekly cyclists is also over 2.1 million, while football is part of the weekly routine for over 1.9 million people.

Other sports becoming more popular – though from a lower base – include boxing and table tennis.

How do people take part?

Sports clubs

Club membership is most common in rugby union and hockey. Over half of those who take part in these sports belong to clubs.

Relatively few people are club members in sports such as athletics (4.7%), swimming (3.1%) and cycling (2.1%).

Club membership has remained fairly the same in most sports since 2007/8.

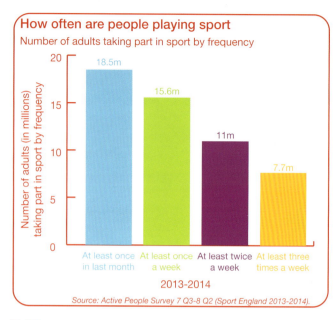

How often are people playing sport

Number of adults taking part in sport by frequency

Number of adults (in millions) taking part in sport by frequency

- At least once in last month: 18.5m
- At least once a week: 15.6m
- At least twice a week: 11m
- At least three times a week: 7.7m

2013-2014

Source: Active People Survey 7 Q3-8 Q2 (Sport England 2013-2014).

Tuition

More than half of all those taking part in rugby union and hockey have had tuition in their sport.

Since 2007/8, tuition rates have fallen in basketball, canoeing and kayaking, cricket and snowsports. Tuition in swimming has increased.

Competition

More than half of those who take part in hockey and rugby union are involved in competition, as are just under half who play netball. Swimmers and cyclists are least likely to compete, but the number of competitive cyclists is growing.

A number of sports have seen changes in competition rates since 2007/8. There have been declines in sports, including football.

The above information is reprinted with kind permission from Sport England.
© Sport England 2014

www.sportengland.org

Mini glossary

Socio-economic groups – *dividing the working population up by what type of job they do (e.g. one group who do manual labour, like electricians or carpenters, whereas another group would be classed as 'professionals', such as teachers and bank managers).*

Ten life skills sport can give you

Confidence, discipline and health for life. Just a few of the reasons why sport should play a major part in your life.

By Keith Kendrick

Once again, it has been an incredible summer of sport.

From the football World Cup, to Wimbledon, to the Commonwealth Games, we just can't get enough of watching in awe as the world's elite sportsmen and women perform for our pleasure. How inspiring was Germany's 7-1 humbling of host nation Brazil, for example? How heart-warming was 13-year-old Erraid Davies's bronze medal in the Commonwealth swimming pool? How awesome was Novak Djokovic's destruction of the incredible Roger Federer?

Be it football or rugby, tennis or badminton, swimming or cycling, gymnastics or – er – darts (yes darts, but more of that later), getting involved with sport will equip you with skills that will set you up for life.

Okay, not everyone can win the World Cup, or Wimbledon or an Olympic or Commonwealth gold, silver or bronze medal, but there's way more to sport than finishing top. You know the saying 'It's the taking part that counts'? Well this isn't altogether true: 'It's COMPETING that counts, aka Trying Your Best.' Competition teaches us about the world beyond childhood more than anything. It shows you that putting in maximum effort and trying to be as good as you can be will reap rewards; but it also teaches you that life is sometimes grossly unfair – because no matter how much effort you put in, sometimes there's always a bigger, stronger, faster, uglier bar-steward who can put you in your place (see 'Brazil-Germany' above!).

But competitiveness isn't the only life skill playing sport can give you. Sports, whether team-based or individual, are great activities that provide a variety of benefits other than physical activity. Participation in sports can help build self-esteem and confidence, can motivate you to excel academically and can help build social skills. Here are ten more life skills – and the sports that best show these benefits:

parentdish
because children don't come with instructions

1. Active lifestyle for life

Too many young people spend a ludicrous amount of time watching TV or playing video games, partly because (it has to be said) TV and video games are fun, but also because many school playing fields have been sold off. It's one of the reasons why we have a childhood obesity crisis. Organised sport participation is the remedy. So, once you get into the habit of running, jumping, sweating and having a great time, you never lose it.

Best sports: Any (with the exception of darts and snooker!).

2. Getting along with people

The world wide web has loads of social media platforms where you can interact with people, such as Snapchat, Twitter and Facebook, but why be a keyboard warrior when you can have real-time interaction with real flesh and blood human beings? Sport is brilliant way to develop social skills that will benefit you throughout your entire life. You can learn to interact with other children your age, and also with older individuals like your coaches and sports officials. You learn leadership skills, team-building skills and communication skills that will help you in school, your future career and personal relationships.

Think about it: the best teams – football, rugby, hockey, you name it – thrive on communication. The most successful have vocal players who are constantly talking to each other about where they're at and where they should be; anticipating problems, admonishing mistakes.

Best sports: Football, rugby, hockey, netball, basketball.

3. Confidence

If you've ever scored a goal, netted a ball, hit a six, whacked an Ace, scored a home run or won a race, you'll know the feeling well: supreme confidence, aka 'Top of the Worldness'. There is no feeling like it.

Look at the reaction of England's Adam Jameli in the 2014 Commonwealth Games 100 metre sprint. He was bursting with pride, bouncing with confidence – and he 'only' won silver. That's what sport gives you: the feeling you can conquer anything – even if you haven't!

4. Setbacks and attacks

Sport isn't all about winning – losing is a huge part of the experience too (I speak with wisdom, believe me). But what do sportspeople do when they miss a penalty or fail to save one? Hide under their duvets, cry into their pillows and refuse to come out to play ever again? Nope, none of that self-pitying nonsense. Sportsfolks dust themselves down, choke back the disappointment and get back onto the field or track to try again.

Setbacks are a great skin-thickening rite of passage. They teach you that nothing is forever; that disappointments are as fleeting as triumphs. And that criticism – ideally constructive – is there to help improve you. Imagine having that attitude to life when something doesn't quite work out the way you would have liked in the classroom? Imagine the stead the thickness of that skin will set you in.

5. Dealing with authority

I'm stating the obvious, but we're all different and have different points of view – and that's a valuable lesson we can learn from sport. There is no better illustration of this fact than the conflict created by a referee's disputed decision. The petulant throw their arms up in horror and continue to protest; the mature get on with the game knowing that the referee is not only unlikely to change his mind – but simply won't. Ever. Wind your neck in and get on with your job.

6. Managing conflict

How on Earth do rugby players manage to stay friends after a match in which they pretty much try to tear the heads off each other's shoulders in the pursuit of victory? Why do boxers hug each other after punching each other in the face as hard as they can for half an hour? Because it's all part of the sport. They know it isn't personal. They appreciate that the other guy is just doing their job, no matter how battered and bruised that other guy has left them. Hell, they even manage to be friends afterwards.

7. Concentration, focus and 'never-say-die' attitude

The elite tennis players are probably the most focused, single-minded sportspeople in the world. Global superstars like Rafael Nadal, Novak Djokovic, Roger Federer don't play a 'match' as such – they play every point. Every single point is a new beginning for them. This is how they manage to come back from two sets down to win 3-2 when us mere mortals would have thrown in the towel at the end of the second set. Yet at the same time, they always have the big picture – the result of the match – in mind. Such skills would be a boon for anyone in life: live in the moment, one step at a time, but without ever losing focus of what you're trying to achieve long term.

8. Sense of identity

It doesn't matter whether you are fat, thin, tall or short, when you pull on your team's shirt, you are part of a family: you belong.

A rugby-playing friend of mine told me how he moved to Canada when he was a teenager and didn't know a soul. All that changed the moment he joined an amateur rugby club. 'I went into the dressing room and instantly had 20 new friends,' he said.

9. How to follow the rules

Sport isn't anarchistic. It's based on agreed rules that all participants accept and abide by (okay, sometimes they're disputed, but let's move on), pretty much as we (most of us) abide by the laws of society. This is a great life skill to learn as early as possible: that not everyone in life revolves around you and your desires; that you need to fit in and play the game (unless you own the ball, in which case you can always take it home if things aren't going your way).

10. Self-discipline

To be good at sport you will need to get up in the morning to be at a certain place at a certain time, you will need to keep yourself in shape so you won't be embarrassed on the park when you play your rivals. These are life skills the modern workplace demands too.

14 August 2014

www.parentdish.co.uk

Mini glossary

Anarchistic – *Refers to anarchy. A state of society without any law or rules that usually leads to confusion and disorder.*

Petulant – *describes someone who is bad-tempered and complaining.*

Bridlington pupil picks up national sports award from Sir Steve Redgrave

Sir Steve Redgrave visited Burlington Junior School in Bridlington today to celebrate the success of the Sporting Promise programme by joining 80 pupils in a sports festival and presenting one lucky pupil with a special national award.

Ten-year-old Elliot Hatton from Bridlington, scooped the first ever Sporting Promise Outstanding Young Person Award, which recognised his commitment to helping others at his school. Burlington received the visit from Sir Steve, who presented Elliot with the achievement, as a prize for him winning the great award.

Cricket-mad Elliot, who captains the under-11's team at Sewerby Cricket Club, was so excited to meet the Olympic hero: 'It has been absolutely amazing to have a true sporting legend give me an award – I won't ever forget it! I'm so thankful to my teachers and my family for their support over the past year – they have been brilliant.'

The Sporting Promise is an award-winning grassroots sports initiative that has already impacted over two million young people in the first three years of the programme. It is a partnership between Sporting Pro, Matalan and the Youth Sport Trust that ensures children across the country have vital access to sports activity in school.

This new award was designed to reflect the powerful impact that sport can have on young people in primary and secondary schools across the country and Elliot was nominated by his teacher, Kerry Scruton, who has been so inspired by Elliot:

'The most rewarding part of my job is seeing transformational change in a young person. Last year, Elliot was having some difficulties at home and in school. His dad became ill and around the same time, some of his friends started bullying him – he lost all confidence and self-esteem and become very negative about school.'

'We chose Elliot to be a Sporting Promise sports leader at the school, as we thought it would help build his confidence. He was proud to have been chosen – it rebuilt his self-assurance and self-belief and also meant that he developed positive friendships with different groups of children. The change we have all seen in Elliot since he became a sports leader is unbelievable – he is now communicating much better and is much more positive about school.'

As part of the prize, Elliot received £200 in Sporting Pro vouchers, while his school received a cheque for £1,000.

Whilst visiting the school, Sir Steve took part in activities that develop the skills young people need for sport including everything from object control with football and hockey activities to target throws with tennis equipment. He was particularly impressed by Elliot's story:

'This just shows the powerful part that sport can play in the lives of young people. It was fantastic to meet with Elliot and his friends today and see the enthusiasm they have for all these sports activities. The support of brands like Sporting Pro and Matalan to fund these programmes is vital to ensure all young people have a range of opportunities to take part and enjoy sport.'

There are three key focus areas for Sporting Promise. TOP Sport supports the delivery of PE and sport in 10,000 primary schools across the country. yoUR Activity promotes the alternative sports offer in secondary schools and Sporting Communities opens up sports opportunities for 14- to 19-year-olds by setting up community sports clubs. Go to www.sportingpromise.co.uk for more details.

9 October 2014

www.youthsporttrust.org

Mini glossary

Grassroots – *refers to involving the common people/ ordinary people.*

Initiative – *introduction (a fresh approach) of an idea or plan to help improve a situation.*

PE and sport premium: more children benefiting from school sport

New research has shown the Government's £150 million a year PE and sport premium is helping to improve primary school sports provision.

Nine out of ten primary schools have improved the quality of PE lessons thanks to the £150 million PE and sport premium, new research has shown.

The fund, introduced in 2013, goes directly to primary school headteachers, who can use it however they want, to provide PE and sporting activities for pupils.

Today's (9 September 2014) figures show that schools are getting real value for money, helping more children get active and healthy, and learning the confidence and skills that will help them to succeed in life.

Schools have used the money to recruit more PE teachers and sports specialists to improve the quality of lessons or after-school clubs, buy new equipment, offer a wider selection of sports and free after-school clubs.

The findings include:

➢ 91% of schools reported an increase in the quality of PE teaching thanks to the funding, with the remainder reporting quality remained the same

➢ 96% of schools reported improvements in pupils' physical fitness, 93% saw improvements in behaviour and 96% thought the funding had contributed to a healthier lifestyle for their pupils

➢ the proportion of schools using specialist PE teachers in lessons rose from 22% to 54%

➢ schools with a high proportion of free school meals (FSM) pupils were more likely to report improvements – 51% of schools with more than a quarter of FSM pupils reported an increase in available facilities compared to 39% of schools with the lowest level of FSM

➢ 84% of schools reported an increase in pupil engagement with PE during school time and 83%

saw an increase in participation in after-school clubs

- ➤ around three quarters of schools used the premium to buy new equipment (76%) or provide more after-school sports clubs (74%)
- ➤ more than two thirds of schools (67%) increased the number of sports offered during lessons with 77% increasing the sports on offer during after-school clubs
- ➤ 63% of schools had increased the amount of competitive sport they play with other schools
- ➤ a third of schools used the premium to reduce the costs of after-schools clubs while a fifth made some clubs completely free to attend.

Education Secretary Nicky Morgan and Children and Families Minister Edward Timpson joined Olympic gold medallist and London 2012 cycling star Victoria Pendleton for a visit to Bacons College, Rotherhithe, where they saw first-hand the benefits of competitive sport.

The group met children from local primary schools trying their hand at a range of sports before meeting some of Bacon College's stars of the future – including the winners of the London Youth Games 4 x 100m relay, an aspiring Chelsea footballer and a nationally ranked badminton player.

Education Secretary Nicky Morgan said:

'We want to create a world-class education system that gives children all the skills they need to succeed in modern Britain. Literacy and numeracy are part of that but confidence, discipline and determination are equally important.

'Some of those things can be taught in the classroom but the lessons children learn while playing sport, such as the importance of teamwork and the satisfaction of achieving a goal, are invaluable.

'I'm delighted the PE and sport premium is having a positive effect on sports in our schools. Whether you're an Olympic champion or a park runner, sport really can change people's lives and I want everyone to take part.'

Olympic gold medallist Victoria Pendleton said:

'Developing a love of sport early on goes a long way to helping children develop confidence and competence.

'Whether it's a netball tournament between a few local schools or being part of an after-school football club, competitive sport really helps children learn resilience,

teamwork and builds character – not to mention the clear benefits for their health.

'Sport at school shouldn't be sidelined – which is why the extra funding primary schools are getting for sport will make such a valuable difference.'

The PE and sport premium was launched in 2013 providing over £150 million a year to improve the quality of provision in every state primary school in England until the 2015 to 2016 financial year. The funding goes directly to primary school headteachers so that they can decide how best to use it to provide PE and sporting activities for pupils.

A typical primary school with 250 primary-age pupils this year received £9,250, the equivalent of around 2 days a week of a primary teacher's or a coach's time.

The fund has been used to:

- ➤ upskill teachers to improve the quality of sport lessons and invest in quality coaching
- ➤ provide more opportunities for pupils to take part in inter-school competitions and offer more after-school clubs
- ➤ purchase better equipment
- ➤ introduce new and unusual sports as diverse as fencing, climbing, and ultimate Frisbee and Danish long-ball to encourage more children to enjoy sport
- ➤ improve sport teaching for children with special educational needs.

The research report, published today (9 September 2014), was based on a survey of primary schools between April and July 2014. It looked at how headteachers have spent the money and the impact of that spending on schools.

The full report is available on GOV.UK (https://www.gov.uk/government/publications/pe-and-sport-premium-an-investigation-in-primary-schools).

9 September 2014

www.gov.uk

Boost for disability sport

One of the guiding principles of the Olympics is the importance of participation as opposed to winning.

'The essential thing is not to have conquered but to have fought well,' said the father of the modern Olympic movement, Baron Pierre de Coubertin.

Paralympians are living examples of people who have triumphed over difficult situations and 'fought well'.

Every Paralympian has an inspirational story to tell. Most people would be impressed and inspired by the sight of an athlete with missing limbs sprinting faster than most able-bodied people.

Read inspiring stories from Paralympians:

➢ **David Weir** (http://www.nhs.uk/LiveWell/fitness/Pages/david-weir-paralympics.aspx)
➢ **Sarah Storey** (http://www.nhs.uk/Livewell/olympics/Pages/sarah-storey.aspx)
➢ **Ian Rose** (http://www.nhs.uk/Livewell/olympics/Pages/Ianrose.aspx)
➢ **David Roberts** (http://www.nhs.uk/Livewell/olympics/Pages/Davidroberts.aspx).

The British Paralympic Association (BPA) hopes that the London 2012 Games will continue to inspire disabled people of all ages to take up sport, either competitively or for its health benefits.

The BPA's Parasport website (www.paralympics.org.uk) aims to increase participation in disability sport by directing people to suitable sports, opportunities, clubs and facilities in their area.

The Parasport website is designed to improve access to regional sports facilities for disabled people.

'Many young people do not know how to access sport for the disabled in their local area,' said a Parasport spokesman. 'Equally, we needed to find new athletes for the GB team in time for 2012 and beyond. We hope this scheme helps to extend the talent pool.'

Britain's got talent

Britain has one of the best records at the Paralympic Games, which were first held in 1960 in Rome. The BPA wants Britain to continue to set the standards in disability sport internationally and to nurture new talent.

The Parasport website is the first of its kind in the UK. Its goal is to inspire anyone with a disability to lead an active lifestyle and enjoy the benefits of participating in sport, such as health, inclusion and social development.

The website has a number of features, including a self-assessment wizard, which allows the user to enter their disability and find suitable sports to participate in. There is information on all the different parasports, videos, photographs and regular news updates.

While the Paralympic sports are at the forefront of disability sporting opportunities, there are plenty of non-Paralympic sports available too. The disability world has a wide variety of sports, including zone hockey, transplant sports, water-skiing, angling, wheelchair dance, hand cycling, motor sports, inclusive gyms and much more.

With its growing clubs and events database, the Parasport website will support and develop as many of these sporting opportunities as possible.

Baroness Tanni Grey-Thompson, Britain's most successful wheelchair athlete, believes the Parasport website will increase the opportunities available to disabled people throughout the UK.

'We want to encourage more youngsters, as well as the disabled community as a whole, to take up sport either competitively or for health reasons,' she says.

1 July 2013

www.nhs.uk

Mini glossary

Forefront – *the leading position.*

Out in Sport

LGBT students' experiences of sport.

Participation in sport

The majority of LGBT students participate in sport or fitness activities of some type, although the type of sport and activity varies across sexual orientation and gender identity.

➤ 59.1 per cent of LGBT students participate in an individual sport or fitness activity, 34.6 per cent participate in an organised team sport and 23.0 per cent participate in an informal team sport. Lesbian women are much more likely than any other group to participate in an organised team sport, with 52.0 per cent of respondents doing so.

➤ Running is the most common form of sporting activity overall, with 18.8 per cent of respondents participating. Going to the gym is more popular with gay and bisexual men, while rugby is more popular with lesbian women.

➤ Most LGBT students are participating in sport organised by their students' union (50.9 per cent) or their university/college (27.1 per cent).

Experiences in sport

Many LGBT students who participate in sport have a positive experience while doing so.

➤ Nearly two thirds (62.2 per cent) of LGBT students who participate in team sport are open about their sexual orientation or gender identity to their team-mates and coaches.

➤ 17.1 per cent of LGBT students who participate in team sport are not open to anyone. The main reason for this was that they do not think it is relevant, but 20.5 per cent of those who are not out are worried it might result in verbal or physical abuse on account of homophobia, transphobia or biphobia.

➤ Only about a third of LGBT students (36.6 per cent) agreed or strongly agreed that equality policies with regards to sport were visible at their institution.

Barriers to participation

Although many LGBT students who do not participate in sport are simply not interested or do not have the time, the research has identified that there are clear cultural, structural and physical barriers that prevent some LGBT students from participating in sport.

➤ 46.8 per cent of LGBT students who do not participate in sport find the culture around sport alienating or unwelcoming.

➤ 41.9 per cent had a negative experience at school which has meant that they don't want to get involved at college or university.

➤ 14.3 per cent had experienced homophobia, biphobia or transphobia which has put them off from participating.

➤ 18.7 per cent were put off by gendered sports teams and this rose to 38.9 per cent of trans respondents.

➤ 9.4 per cent were put off by gender-specific kit and/or clothing and this rose to 36.1 per cent for trans respondents.

➤ 12.8 per cent do not find the facilities, such as showers or changing rooms, inclusive and this rose to 36.1 per cent for trans respondents.

Making sport more inclusive

LGBT students have clear opinions on the way that sport can be made more inclusive.

➤ The most popular suggestion for encouraging more LGBT people to be involved in sport was tackling homophobia/transphobia/biphobia in sport within schools, which received the support of 48.3 per cent of LGBT students.

➤ There was also a lot of support for celebrating LGBT role models in sport; training for staff and coaches; training for sports societies; a clear and visible equality policy; having more mixed-gender sports teams; and ensuring facilities are gender neutral.

Recommendations

For sports teams and societies

Sports teams and societies and others who are directly involved in the delivery of sporting experiences for students should:

➤ **Publicise LGBT-friendliness:** In order to create an environment that is welcoming to LGBT students, sports teams and societies should publicly demonstrate their inclusiveness, such as through the Government's charter for action on tackling homophobia, biphobia and transphobia in sport.

➤ **Adopt a zero tolerance to homophobia policy:** Sports teams and societies need to be clear that homophobic, biphobic and transphobic abuse is unacceptable through a clear zero tolerance policy. This will help to ensure that LGBT students feel safe to participate in sport.

➤ **Provide guidance for trans students:** Sports teams and societies should make available a clear and easily-accessible policy on whether, and under what conditions, trans students are eligible to participate and/or compete in sport.

For students' unions

Students' unions, providers of further and higher education, national governing bodies of sport, and others who provide and regulate sport for students should:

➤ **Provide more mixed-gender sporting options:** Students' unions and others that provide and regulate sport should make more mixed-gender teams available in order to reduce the effects of gender stereotypes in sport and allow LGBT students to feel more comfortable participating.

➤ **Audit sports facilities:** Students should have the option of single-cubicle, gender-neutral facilities such as showers and changing rooms. Educational institutions and others providing sports facilities should audit their existing facilities to assess how inclusive they are and include LGBT students in this process. New facilities should be built with the express purpose of being inclusive to all.

➤ **Train sports teams and societies:** Students' unions and others organising the provision of sport should provide training that enables sports teams and societies to create a welcoming, supportive environment where LGBT students feel comfortable being open about their sexual orientation or gender identity and empowers them to eliminate homophobia, transphobia and biphobia from sport.

➤ **Train coaches and other sports staff:** Organisations that provide and regulate sport should provide training for coaches and staff on how to lead LGBT-positive environments. Organisations involved in the training of coaches should incorporate LGBT issues into their training provision.

➤ **Support and celebrate LGBT role models:** Only athletes themselves can decide whether to be open about their sexuality, but organisations providing sporting opportunities should support those who do come out and celebrate them as role models, whether on a national or local level. Organisations should strive to create an atmosphere in which athletes are comfortable and supported in being open about their sexuality.

For schools

Schools and other providers of sports activities for under-16-year-olds should:

➤ **Teach LGBT-inclusiveness:** Schools and other providers of sports activities for under-16-year-

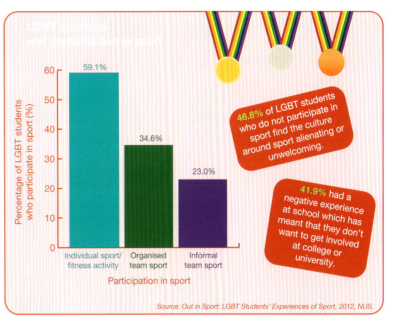

46.8% of LGBT students who do not participate in sport find the culture around sport alienating or unwelcoming.

41.9% had a negative experience at school which has meant that they don't want to get involved at college or university.

Source: Out in Sport: LGBT Students' Experiences of Sport, 2012, NUS.

olds should use sport as a way to teach children that homophobia, biphobia and transphobia are unacceptable and that all members of a sports team should contribute to creating an inclusive environment.

➤ **Encourage a broad range of sporting activities:** Schools and other providers of sports activities should make an effort to support students to participate in a broad range of sports, including those that are not typical for their gender.

The above information is reprinted with kind permission from the National Union of Students (NUS). © NUS 2014

www.nus.org.uk

Mini glossary

Biphobia/biphobic – people who have a fear and hatred of bisexuals (people who are attracted to both sexes).

Eligible – if someone meets a certain set of criteria then they will be allowed participate.

Homophobia/homophobic – people who have a fear and hatred of homosexuals (people who are attracted to members of the same sex).

Transphobia/transphobic – people who have a fear and hatred of transsexuals (people who identify with a gender that is not culturally associated with their sex assigned at birth).

Adapting sports to lifestyles of girls and women is key

Women's participation in sport

Almost without exception, women and girls are less likely to participate in sport than men. Women's sport has for too long been seen as an add-on to men's sport, of less interest to both male and female spectators and even, among some people, as unfeminine.

Girls give up sport at an earlier age than boys, and are less likely than men to sustain participation into adulthood, as other responsibilities reduce leisure time. Even for those who do want to continue to participate, there are problems of accessibility, availability of suitable facilities and cost.

Women's sport and the media

At elite level, there has been a reluctance in the media to cover women's sport. This has discouraged potential interest among spectators and possible commercial sponsors, which in turn has led to low interest amongst the media. This situation was already changing before the 2012 Olympics and Paralympics, but the successes of UK sportswomen in 2012 have given the media motivation to cover women's sport.

However, more work is needed to strengthen the circle of good media coverage/higher spectator or viewer engagement/greater sponsorship and a more attractive product/greater media interest.

Recommendations

➢ In schools, the Committee recommends co-operation with other providers to make a wider range of sports and fitness activities available, better training for PE teachers, a more equal distribution of finance between boys' and girls' sport and better facilities – especially changing facilities.

➢ Even where facilities are available, not enough thought is often given to the needs of women or groups of women: for example, sports halls are built with public viewing galleries or women-only swimming sessions are patrolled by male lifeguards, which means that Muslim women and others with similar cultural restrictions cannot participate.

➢ The Committee believes that there should be an additional target in the Government's Youth and Community Strategy for increasing the participation of women and girls, but to avoid over-burdening sports with too many potentially conflicting requirements – it should be imposed only on

those NGBs that are not seriously addressing the potential for growing women's participation in their sport.

➢ As far as elite sport is concerned, the Committee noted a number of initiatives by NGBs to attract greater media coverage and/or commercial sponsorship, some of which involved linking women's sport to the men's game (for example, holding women's Six Nations rugby matches just before or just after the men's equivalent), some to marketing the sport in a completely new way (such as netball), some to moving fixtures to a time when it was easier for broadcasters to cover them more extensively (such as the women's FA Cup Final). The Committee believed there was scope for more sports to adapt in this way, and also to promote their sportswomen and to provide commentary and narratives in a way more likely to engage the media and therefore public attention.

➢ However, efforts also needed to be made by the media and commercial sponsors, who – the Committee considered – were missing an underdeveloped marketing opportunity by failing to engage with women's sport. The Committee urged national newspapers to publish the results of women's matches alongside the men's, and called on journalists and commentators to refrain from making derogatory (damaging) remarks about the sportswomen.

Coaching

One area where the presence of women makes a great difference to sportswomen is coaching. It was strongly argued, on the basis of both surveys and the experience of elite sportswomen, that women would be encouraged to take part, and persist, in sport were there more female coaches. The sporting authorities are trying to encourage more women to become involved in coaching.

However, not only are women discouraged from becoming coaches by the low pay and long and inflexible hours, but also it appears that some meet with sexism and lack of respect among both players and fellow coaches. If sports governing bodies are serious about encouraging greater participation by women, then they must take action to drive this sort of behaviour out of their sports.

25 July 2014

www.parliament.uk

Sport and faith

On 17 July 2014, the innovative 'Celebrating the Gift in Sport' conference took place. It explored how sport and faith can combine to champion the gifts of each person. Pope Francis' message for the conference showed support for 'everyone who enjoys sport as a means of celebrating the sheer joy of the gift of life and of promoting the dignity and potential of the human person'. This goes to show that faith and sport can work very well together and benefit from each other. In particular, by engaging faith communities in sports, this can help to increase participation in sport and also to promote ethnic diversity across sport and physical activities.

Understanding faith communities

'Faith communities are groupings of people belonging to the major world religions and of those who follow other forms of religious expression'. According to the UK Census 2011, of the UK population who did have a religious affiliation, the majority followed one of six world religions: Christianity (59.3%), Islam/Muslim (4.8%), Hinduism (1.5%), Sikhism (0.8%), Judaism (0.5%) and Buddhism (0.4%). Some religions people identified with do not fall into any of the main religious groups (0.4%), such as Pagan and Spiritualist. 25.1% of people reported that they did not have a religion and 7.2% of people did not answer the question on religious affiliation.

So, how does sport fit into the mix? Well, the strength of the religious community can help to encourage and support participation in sport:

➢ Faith centres have an established connection with a large group of people, which means they have a big reach and influence in the community.

➢ Faith centres are a key resource that can be accessed by many people who may fear cultural or religious barriers from wider society – faith centres already understand and are aware of potential concerns people may have with participating in sport and are obviously more accommodating to a person's faith than wider society would be.

➢ Faith centres have the potential to offer land and facilities for sport. For example, some Hindu temples offer yoga as not only a form of exercise but as a way to link back to the spiritual side of Hinduism.

Barriers to sport participation

There can sometimes be clashes between religion and sport due to a conflict between the rules of sport and some religious beliefs – this can be down to health and safety concerns or because an organisation wishes to remain religiously neutral. Another potential barrier to sport can be down to the fact that some religious people might feel that wider society might not be able to offer suitable facilities which comply with their religious beliefs.

Below are some real life examples of religion/sport conflicts:

FIFA officially allows players to wear religious headgear

FIFA have overturned their ban on most types of headgear for football players. This decision will officially allow Muslim women to wear the hijab, Sikhs to wear the turban and Jewish players to wear the kippah without fear of any rule violation.

Talented Muslim basketball player restricted by hijab ban

Basketball phenomenon, Bilqis Abdul-Qaadir became the first female athlete to play Division I sports – the highest level of sports at the US college level – in full hijab. Abdul-Qaadir, does not wish to compromise her religious beliefs by removing her hijab, as it is a part of who she is. However, the rules of the International Basketball Federation (FIBA) have banned items such as the Islamic headscarf or hijab in an attempt to remain religiously neutral. This means that Abdul-Qaadir, a talented Muslim player, has no chance of pursuing a professional basketball career and playing international basketball. Leading American Muslim advocacy group, Council on American-Islamic Relations (CAIR), has written to FIBA in an attempt to get this rule overturned.

Newcastle striker Papiss Cissé refused to wear sponsored shirt on religious grounds

Back in July 2013, Muslim football player, Papiss Cissé (Newcastle United striker), did not wish to wear the club's new branded kit as it went against the teachings of his religion. This was because the club's sponsor was Wonga, a high interest UK payday loans company, and under Sharia Law Muslims must not benefit from the lending of money. However, after negotiations, Cissé agreed to wear the Wonga-branded kit.

For further information please visit the following sources:

➢ www.scmo.org

➢ www.sportingequals.com

➢ http://www.guardian.co.tt/sport/2014-03-17 headwear-forces-fifa-change-heart

➢ http://www.islamophobiawatch.co.uk/hijab-ban threatens-basketball-phenom/

➢ http://www.theguardian.com/football/2013/jul/25 papiss-cisse-newcastle-wonga-row

The above information is written by Christina Hughes on behalf of Independence Educational Publishers.
© Independence Educational Publishers 2014

Activities

Brainstorm

1. What are the Olympic and Paralympic games, and why are they important?

Oral activities

2. What are the benefits of participating in sport? Discuss this as a class. Hint: think beyond the physical benefits.

3. Divide your class into two groups: boys and girls. In your groups, discuss why you think there are fewer women than men participating in sport. When both groups have a list of ideas, compare your thoughts and discuss the differences in your opinions.

Research activity

4. Pick a sportsperson you admire and research their career. Write a report about why you look up to them and what they have achieved.

Written activities

5. Write a letter to your headteacher, explaining why it is important for your school to encourage young people to participate in sports.

6. What would you change about the sports curriculum in your school? Write a proposal that highlights the changes you would make, and explain why.

Moral dilemma

7. '46.8% of LGBT students who do not participate in sport find the culture around sport alienating or unwelcoming'. How can sport teams help make LGBT students feel safe and encourage them to participate in sport?

Design activities

8. Choose a relatively unknown or unheard of sport. Create an action plan that will encourage the sport to be more widely played in the UK. Your action plan could include posters, a draft TV ad, etc. Present your action plan to the class.

9. Identify the qualities you think a sportsperson should display and create a poster encouraging good sportsmanship and fair play. Which public figures do you think embody good sportsmanship? What about bad/poor sportsmanship?

Are top athletes born or made?

By Mauro van de Looij, Sports & Achievement Psychologist and Child Psychologist.

Have you ever seen the television series Made (MTV)? On this show one person wants to change his or her life and often wants to be 'made' the person of his or her dreams. Remember the girls wanting to be made popstars and the guys sport jocks? Whether you liked the show or not, it was a great format to help people become what they wanted to be. Now, let me ask you a question: do you think it is possible to be made in accordance with your dreams? Do you think top athletes are born or made?

More often than not you hear people credit quality to talent. For example, a football commentator may enthusiastically shout out loud: 'What a goal! This kid is amazingly talented!' Exactly what does talented mean? Does the commentator mean the player has incredible natural abilities which make him such a good striker? I reckon he does. Is he, then, right about attributing this player's quality to born characteristics? I believe he is not. Honestly, I reckon him – and his colleagues – to be way off with such an attribution.

Allow me to clarify myself on this one. First of all I believe your quality as a top athlete to consist of three aspects: natural abilities (talent), ability + motivation to learn and practice time. Natural abilities are of course the gifts you got from your parents (height for example). Ability + motivation to learn are necessary for developing, without it you will not develop (your talent). Practice time is the amount of time spent practising, the more time you spend the higher your quality will be.

Secondly, there is a lot of research that has found effort, practice and learning to be more important than talent (e.g. Jowett & Spray, 2013). In order to make my belief more credible I will discuss two examples that perfectly endorse my view that it takes more, a lot more, than sole talent to become an athlete of world-class status. I bring to you Cristiano Ronaldo and Lionel Messi – considered by many the best football players on the planet at this very moment. A lot of people speak about their giftedness and talent for football. Is that truly all it took them to become world class on the pitch? For my master's research (titled Growth Mindset and Goal Orientations in Football) I took a look at their history and development. As it turns out, both Ronaldo and Messi have walked a similar path to become

the quality players we know now. Heads up: it took them more than just talent!

When they were young they both enjoyed football greatly and had a very strong desire to become a professional football player. Therefore, they have been playing football a lot during their younger years, starting from around the age of five. At about 12 years of age, Ronaldo and Messi left their families for a place in a European Youth Football Academy (Ronaldo – Sporting Lisbon, Messi – FC Barcelona). Besides the shared dream they are also characterized for (and still have) their discipline to make the football dream come true. As opposed to loads of young boys who share the same dream, Ronaldo and Messi showed the discipline necessary in making this dream reality. The discipline consists of training, practising and learning. Throughout their teenage years they cared about, and were busy with, only one thing: the ball.

Were Messi and Ronaldo nothing special when they were young then? Of course they possessed qualities at a young age, otherwise they would not have been given the chance at a European Youth Football Academy. How did they develop then? According to youth coaches, Messi had something special at a young age, though he had a growth hormone deficit meaning his growth was delayed. Within FC Barcelona, controversy existed about Messi and his opportunity to become a professional football player. Eventually they took chances and were the only club willing and able to pay for the medical bills. Messi was offered the opportunity to make his dream come true at La Masia. To make it clear, even at that stage FC Barcelona were all but certain whether Messi could reach the professional football level. Imagine for a second that FC Barcelona had not given Messi that chance, we probably would have never heard of him because he would not have had the opportunity to develop and improve his qualities (and deal with his medical setback). So Messi had to come a long way. Ronaldo stated his mum could have never guessed him to become such a great football player when he was young. This means it has never been a fact that Ronaldo would become one based upon his talent. For both Messi and Ronaldo nobody knew for sure they would be a professional football player in the future. Then what has been the key for Messi and Ronaldo? Practice! According to Ericsson (2006) – who is a psychologist – we need 10,000 hours of deliberate practice to become an expert in that field. If you have a dream, make sure you reach that amount of hours to make it become reality. Now taking this into account, I reckon Ronaldo and Messi have passed this amount of hours easily by now and may even have by their early twenties. Could that be a reason for them winning the Ballon d'Or (Ronaldo – 2008, Messi – 2009, 2010, 2011, 2012)?

According to former teammates, Ronaldo was always the first and the last person on the training ground:

Goalkeeper van der Sar: 'After training he was always practising his free kick. If he needed a goalkeeper, to him I was the only option. If I asked him whether another goalkeeper could defend the goal during his free kick training he replied: "I only want to train with the best so I can become the best." Now that got me motivated alright.'

Former manager Sir Alex Ferguson: 'Ronaldo's discipline was fantastic. I always saw him to be first and last on the pitch. Besides, he wouldn't give 100%, he gave 120%! Every time again.'

Ruud van Nistelrooij who played alongside Ronaldo up front at Man United says: 'He is so complete. He trained and still trains every aspect of the game to become the best he can be. Heading, free kicks, two footedness, corner kicks, everything he practises. He is always training.'

Teammate **Gerard Pique** at FC Barcelona about Lionel Messi: 'Aside from all the talent he's got, it's true that Messi learnt a lot at Barcelona. I don't know if Messi would be what he is today if he had left the club.'

Well, what has been key in becoming world-class players for Ronaldo and Messi? Practice, right! And let me ask you again, do you believe top athletes are born or made? I reckon you will say it is possible to be made into a top athlete. Then why, you might ask, do 'we' attribute quality to talent? How come the commentator shouts out 'what an amazing talented player'? Good question!

The answer, I think, lies in the so-called fundamental attribution error-phenomenon. Did you ever go for lunch and experience the waiter or waitress being unfriendly to you? What attribution did or would you make for this waiter's odd behaviour? Probably you would say this waiter is not a nice guy at all, he might even be a schmuck and not fit for the job like the way he is (not) serving you. This attribution is perfectly understandable as our minds do not have the time, energy or interest to take all circumstances that could influence someone's behaviour into account. However, maybe the waiter had a bad day – he got dumped by his girlfriend, he failed his driving licence test

or has been bothered by other customers all day long – and consequently could not be friendly to you. If you think about such a scenario then can you understand the waiter's behaviour (better). In essence, the waiter's example is exactly what 'we' do regarding athletes. We forget to look to the history and development of top athletes. Don't get me wrong, I understand attributing behaviour (quality on the pitch) to the person (talent) perfectly, but, to say the very least, it hardly ever is the correct attribution to make.

Therefore, try to take circumstances into account, for you may be less frustrated. As for sports, imagine young children playing a nice game of football. If they believe talent is all it takes to become a professional football player, your chances of becoming one are less than 1% or so, for there's always a person out there who's more talented than you are. Therefore you might lose interest, don't try as hard as you could and may even quit playing. Now, if we all start believing and expressing it took the likes of Ronaldo, Messi, Federer, Nadal and Tiger Woods many hours of practice, effort and learning to become such great athletes, maybe our kids will learn to appreciate the value of working hard. Maybe they will add the discipline necessary for their dream to come true. And what is more beautiful than our dreams coming true?

I would like to conclude by stating top athletes are made and never born. However, if you happen to find a baby doing all the tricks our top athletes do nowadays, I am more than interested in hearing more about this little genius. To underline that it takes effort more than talent, I have to confess I have rewritten this article a few times before it went public for you to read. To me, practice does make perfect!

References

➢ Jowett, N. & Spray, C.M. (2013). British Olympic Hopefuls: The antecedents and consequences of implicit ability beliefs in elite track and field athletes. *Psychology of Sport and Exercise*, 14, 145–153.

➢ CNN Documentary about Cristiano Ronaldo – http://www.youtube.com/watch?v=iHkHTpuGaD8.

➢ ITV Documentary about Lionel Messi – http://www.dailymotion.com/video/xpas6i_messi-belgeseli-ingilizce_sport.

6 December 2013

www.thesportinmind.com

Dangers of doping

What's the big deal?

Most medications on the Prohibited List can be bought at a pharmacy – so they must be safe to use, right?

NO! Medications are for people with specific health issues – not healthy athletes. They were not approved to be used by healthy people, in higher doses and in combination with other substances.

What about dietary or nutritional supplements?

'All-natural. Pure fast results.' BEWARE!

Supplement companies are not highly regulated – meaning you never know what you are taking. There could be a banned substance in your 'all-natural' supplement.

What's at risk?

All medications have side effects – but taking them when your body doesn't need them can cause serious damage to your body and destroy your athletic career.

The women all look like men!

And the men look ridiculous!

What else should you know?

Methods

There are also methods of administering substances or manipulating your physiology that are banned. These methods can also have negative effects on your body. For example, blood doping, including having blood transfusions to change the way your blood carries oxygen to the rest of your body, may result in:

➢ An increased risk of heart failure, stroke, kidney damage and high blood pressure
➢ Problems with your blood – like infections, poisoning, overloading of your white cells and reduction of platelet count
➢ Problems with your circulatory system.

HIV/AIDS

As with any injectable drug, using a syringe to dope puts you at a higher risk for contracting infectious diseases such as HIV/AIDS and hepatitis.

What happens to an athlete who uses?

Steroids

Steroids may make your muscles big and strong, BUT… you may become dependent on them and they may:

➢ Give you acne
➢ Make you bald
➢ Increase your risk of liver and cardiovascular disease
➢ Give you mood swings
➢ Make you more aggressive
➢ Make you suicidal.

Guys, you may also look forward to:

➢ Shrinking testicles
➢ Breast growth
➢ Reduced sex drive and even impotence
➢ Decrease in sperm production.

Ladies, you may look forward to:

➢ Deeper voice
➢ Excessive facial and body hair
➢ Abnormal menstrual cycles
➢ An enlarged clitoris.

EPO

EPO (erythropoietin) may help with the way your body uses oxygen, BUT… why risk it when it may lead to death?

Using EPO may make your blood more like honey – thick and sticky – than water. Trying to pump this thick blood through your veins may:

- Make you feel weak – not good when you are trying to train hard!
- Give you high blood pressure
- Make your heart work so hard that you have a heart attack or stroke (even at your age).

Stimulants

Stimulants are used to heighten the competitive edge, BUT… how edgy would you feel if you:

- Can't sleep (insomnia)
- Have involuntary shaking or trembling
- Have problems with your coordination and balance
- Are anxious and aggressive
- Develop an increased and irregular heart rate
- Have a heart attack (imagine dying of a heart attack at your age!) or stroke
- These are the effects that using stimulants may have on your body.

HGH

HGH (human growth hormone) may make muscles and bones stronger and recover faster, BUT… it is not only your muscles that get bigger.

Using HGH may lead to:

- Acromegaly – protruding forehead, brow, skull and jaw – which can't be reversed
- An enlarged heart that can result in high blood pressure and even heart failure
- Damage to your liver, thyroid and vision
- Crippling arthritis.

Masking agents

Some athletes try to cheat the system by using diuretics and other substances to cover-up the signs of using banned substances.

The side effects can definitely affect your ability to compete and train. You may:

- Become dizzy or even faint
- Become dehydrated
- Get muscle cramps
- Have a drop in blood pressure

- Lose coordination and balance
- Become confused and moody
- Develop cardiac disorders.

Marijuana

Marijuana, cannabis, pot – whatever you call it, IT IS BANNED. Whether you are a pot-head or a casual user, marijuana may have a negative effect on your athletic performance and your health.

Using may:

- Reduce your memory, attention and motivations – even result in learning disabilities
- Weaken your immune system
- Affect your lungs (chronic bronchitis and other respiratory diseases, even throat cancer)
- Lead to psychological and physical dependence.

Narcotics

Narcotics, like heroin and morphine, may help you forget about the pain, BUT… how competitive do you think you'd be with a:

- Weakened immune system
- Decreased heart rate and suppressed respiratory system (you can't compete if you are dead)
- Loss in balance, coordination and concentration
- Gastrointestinal problem like vomiting and constipation
- Narcotics are also highly addictive – your body and mind quickly become dependent on them.

World Anti-Doping Agency's (WADA) 'Dangers of Doping Leaflet'. Please note that the original version can be found on WADA's website at the following link: http://www.wada-ama.org/Documents/Education_Awareness/Tools?Dangers_ of_Doping_Leaflet/WADA_Dangers_of_Doping_EN.pdf
© WADA 2014

www.wada-ama.org

Mini glossary

Diuretics – *this is a substance, sometimes called 'water tablets/pills', which increases the amount of urine a person produces. This is done in order to hide banned substances during urine tests, as urine is more diluted. Diuretic use in sporting competitions is illegal.*

Stimulants – *a drug which causes a temporary improvement in mental or physical functioning.*

We don't listen to children when it comes to abuse in sport

THE CONVERSATION

By Jameel Hadi, Lecturer in Social Work at the University of Salford

Sky Sports presenter Charlie Webster has said she revealed details about sexual abuse by her coach when she was young in order to 'break the taboo about abuse as a whole'.

There are certainly issues within sport where too often, poor practice and abuse is tolerated. Who can forget the unravelling of the systematic abuse and cover up of football coach Jerry Sandusky at Penn State and his subsequent jailing for 30 years in 2012?

A series of high-profile cases, including a British Olympic swimming coach convicted for two rapes, and reports did lead to a change in official procedures and the creation of the NSPCC Child Protection in Sport Unit in 2001. This has driven the adoption of safeguarding standards within sport. But there is no evidence that this process has led to an increased awareness by children about their rights, the behaviour they should expect from adults and who they should turn to if they experience abuse.

A recent study, published by researchers from Edinburgh University and the NSPCC, found that although 'participating in organised sport is a positive experience for most children and young people … a negative sporting culture exists, is accepted "as the norm" and is perpetuated by peers, coaches and other adults.' The study reported widespread emotionally harmful treatment (75%) and unacceptable levels of sexual harassment (29%).

There are still plenty of anecdotal accounts of children experiencing bullying, adult pressure and exclusion, which has resulted in the Football Association's Respect campaign and grassroots campaigns such as Give us Back our Game.

The implementation of the Children Act 2004 gave emphasis to safeguarding within sport, particularly as this made it clear that promoting the welfare of children was not simply a professional task but the responsibility of all adults, many of whom in sport act in a voluntary capacity. A network of welfare officers now exist on a national, regional and club level in order to promote best practice and to provide a mechanism to deal with complaints or concerns.

For many children sport is a chance to be with friends and experience freedom away from the confines of school or home. This has associated benefits as children who take part in organised activities are more likely to experience a sense of well-being and achieve success. And participating in sports promotes resilience and self-sufficiency. But the way they experience sport is shaped by adults who determine the content, rules and expectations.

Celia Brackenridge, the foremost authority on child protection in sport, said, 'Social control is adeptly applied in youth sport where adults choose, organise, deliver and evaluate activities without inviting comments or contributions from those who consume them – children.'

Being on the winning team

The culture of denial and silence is rooted in the reality that children's sport replicates the professional game where winning is the prime motivation. This means that children compete for spaces in teams and at the elite end are under pressure to conform in order not to undermine their prospects of future success. In this context, to speak out is to risk being left out or incur the displeasure of the coach. A recent *Guardian* article brought into sharp focus the contrast between the glitter of the Premier League when compared to what it termed 'the abuse, death threats, and withering numbers in grassroots football'.

And inevitably, a culture of denial or silence means that bullying, shouting and criticism, exclusion and hostility to opponents can go unchallenged. In Canada when a series of sexual abuse cases came to light in ice hockey, it was found that parent after parent was suspicious of the coach's behaviour and attitude but buried their concerns for fear of scuppering their children's chance at success. On a more routine level, there is a resigned acceptance that poor behaviour and unfair practice is just part of the deal.

Policy vacuum

There is a policy vacuum at national and local level. In 2010 the FA conducted a consultation that suggested that many young people had little or no knowledge of the FA's safeguarding procedures or where they could get more information, advice and support.

Rectifying this will involve creating a culture where young people feel able to set their own priorities. The FA's consultation on youth football included a series of road shows entitled Your Kids, Your Say. But where are the children's voices in this?

Some good things have been happening. A project developed by PTS undertook work on behalf of organisations including the FA, British Judo and Sports Leaders UK to capture the voices of children and resulted in training materials and a film that focused on young people's priorities, such as more say in decisions usually the preserve of adults, such as choosing the captain of a team. The film featured a coach patting all his players on the back after a penalty shootout but ignoring the child who missed the penalty that lost the game. One leading coach said the film should 'have adults squirming on their backsides'.

PTS also developed a model of youth leadership, and a children's consultation that identified what was important to children about being in sport and how this related to

policies to keep them safe. Children who participated in an FA conference said they wanted an environment of fun, friendship, inclusion and safety that takes precedence over a competitive adult agenda.

One ten-year-old said: 'The quality of relationships and experience is more important than the outcome.' Listening to and involving children is fundamental to ensuring that children speak out. If children are involved in decisions, they are more likely to trust adults and voice concerns.

21 February 2014

> *The above information is reprinted with kind permission from The Conversation. © 2010-2014, The Conversation Trust (UK)*

www.theconversation.com

Mini glossary

Anecdotal account – *evidence based on a personal account, a person telling their side of an event.*

Perpetuated – *made worse by.*

Resilience – *the ability to return to normal and bounce-back from a setback.*

Too many foreign signings, say football fans

By Chris Polechonski

This week Arsenal midfielder Jack Wilshere made comments in which he stated that 'the only people who should play for England are English people'. This was followed today by a new 'State of the Game' study from the BBC, showing that English footballers play less than one third of all the minutes in the Premier League.

New YouGov research, carried out following the closure of the most recent transfer window, reveals that more than three quarters of football fans (78%) think Premier League clubs are signing too many foreign players. Only 6% disagree.

Similarly, nearly four in five fans (79%) believe there should be a limit on the number of foreign players a Premier League team has in their match-day squad, while about one in six (16%) say there should not be a cap.

The research suggests football fans agree with previous concerns expressed by FA Chairman, Greg Dyke, about the impact overseas players are having in the top flight on the national game.

10 October 2013

www.yougov.co.uk

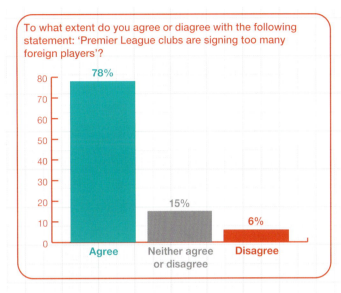

To what extent do you agree or diagree with the following statement: 'Premier League clubs are signing too many foreign players'?

Agree — 78%
Neither agree or disagree — 15%
Disagree — 6%

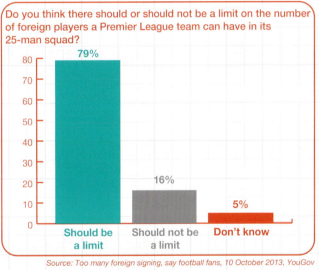

Do you think there should or should not be a limit on the number of foreign players a Premier League team can have in its 25-man squad?

Should be a limit — 79%
Should not be a limit — 16%
Don't know — 5%

Source: Too many foreign signing, say football fans, 10 October 2013, YouGov

Racism in football exists – but do fans think it's a problem?

91% of football fans in England think racism exists in football – the second highest in Europe – but they are amongst the least likely to say it is a serious problem.

By Luke Chambers

YouGov interviewed fans and the general public in England, Scotland, France, Germany, Spain, Italy and The Netherlands about their attitudes to racism and homophobia in football.

Reports from fans across Europe consistently show that racism exists in football. Italian football tops the league, with 92% of fans saying it exists in Italian football. England is a close second with 91%, with Spanish fans reporting the lowest incidence of racism, with 73% feeling that it exists.

Of those who say that racism exists, English fans are amongst the least likely to view the problem as serious (43%). Scottish fans are the least likely to see racism as a serious problem (38%), with Italian fans the most likely (71%).

The issue has recently become of importance in Italian football. In January, former AC Milan forward Kevin-Prince Boateng became the first player to walk off the pitch in response to racist chanting, with the game later abandoned. Since then a referee has stopped a match between AC Milan and Roma in response to the problem, and Lazio were forced to close a stand of their stadium for the opening weekend of the Italian season following persistent problems.

English fans give clubs and players the most credit for combating racism, with 40% feeling that they are doing enough. Despite this, every football authority put to English fans was judged to not be doing enough to combat racism. Just 17% of English fans feel that international authorities such as FIFA and UEFA are doing enough.

Across Europe, football fans feel that players, clubs, national and international governing bodies and fans themselves are not doing enough to combat the problem. On average across the seven countries surveyed, only 22% of fans feel that the international bodies such as UEFA and FIFA are doing enough to tackle racism.

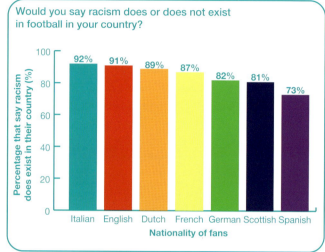

Would you say racism does or does not exist in football in your country?

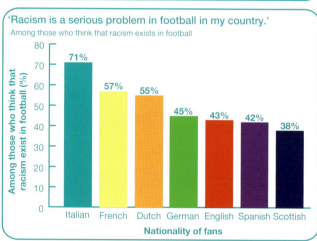

'Racism is a serious problem in football in my country.'
Among those who think that racism exists in football

Source: Racism in football exists – but do fans think it's a problem?, 16 September 2013, YouGov

FIFA President Sepp Blatter caused controversy in 2011 by suggesting race-related incidents could be settled with a post-match handshake; meanwhile Head of UEFA Michel Platini stated any player walking off the pitch at Euro 2016 because of racist chanting would be booked.

16 September 2013

www.yougov.co.uk

Match-fixing creates a dark cloud over English football

A dark cloud has descended over the beautiful game in recent weeks as several match-fixing scandals spread across the news.

By Ellen Farrell

As the days go by, more and more scandals are being brought to the public's attention with former AC Milan player, Gattuso, the most recent high-profile footballer to have allegedly been involved in match-fixing in Serie A.

This follows on from Sam Sodje, an ex-Portsmouth player, telling an undercover reporter he could arrange yellow and red cards in exchange for money and Blackburn's DJ Campbell being arrested along with six other people in connection with allegations of match and spot-fixing.

This is not the first time that a match-fixing scandal has plagued the world of football. Just in February of this year, Europol identified 380 matches in Europe which were claimed to have been fixed and a further 300 more around the world. Their investigation recognised 425 suspects and 50 people were arrested. There was even the allegation by a Turkish official that the Champions League, Europe's most prestigious club competition, was fixed by using vibrating balls for the draw.

Match-fixing is a serious criminal problem which is a threat to the integrity and reputation of sport and is a growing concern within football. The commercialisation and globalisation of football has arguably transformed it into a marketable commodity, making it attractive for big investors who perceive it as an enterprise where money can be generated and footballing empires created. However, the presence of capitalism and commercialism in football has fuelled the proliferation of money-making motives and match-fixing provides an opportunity for a lot of money to be made.

Out of the 380 suspicious European matches identified in the Europol investigation, more than £8 million was generated in betting profits and more than £2 million was paid in bribes. Footballers themselves can make money from it, especially through spot-fixing where they manipulate a certain aspect of the game. Players become greedy and therefore may happily accept money for arranging to help fix matches despite their large wage packets. Former Southampton player Matt Le Tissier admitted taking part in a bet which could have netted him £10,000 for kicking the ball out of play at a certain time in a premier league match against Wimbledon in 1995.

Match-fixing challenges and undermines the fundamental values which sport prides itself upon such as fair play, respect and honesty. Moreover, it sabotages the exciting and uncertain element of surprise that sport creates and so football is in danger of becoming a corrupt institution.

A leading FIFA official, Jerome Valcke, labelled match-fixing a disease which could kill the sport if nothing is done to eradicate it. FIFA has recognised the threat that match-fixing poses to the integrity of football and has recently launched a £17.5 million ten-year partnership with Interpol in a bid to combat it.

It is vital that this dark cloud is lifted but, as recent events demonstrate, more needs to be done to fight the 'disease' which is contaminating football before it kills the beautiful game.

24 December 2013

www.offsiderulepodcast.com

Mini glossary

Allegation – *a claim that someone has done something wrong or illegal.*

Sabotages – *ruin on purpose. If something is sabotaged it is destined for failure.*

eSports: a new kind of sport

By Julian del Prado

There has always been debate about what qualifies as a sport. Is golf really a sport? Or is it just a game, since the people involved aren't exerting themselves as much as, say, basketball players. Chess is often called a sport, and yet the entire event takes place sitting down. Even curling, an Olympic sport, is often ridiculed for bringing slightly overweight middle-aged contestants to the same event as gymnastic Olympians.

And then there are eSports. Online games that resemble sports in their construction are becoming an international phenomenon, and they challenge many assumptions about spectator sports.

While eSports flourished in Asia far before they did in the United States, the release of StarCraft II in 2010 catalysed the meteoric rise of eSports in North America. As the game gained more players and a base of viewers willing to watch streams of semi-professional and professional players, the stage was set for an even bigger eSport: League of Legends (LoL). Not only is LoL free to play, it's one of the biggest video games on Earth with 27 million daily players and 67 million monthly players.

In 2013, the LoL World Championship netted 34 million viewers, making it the biggest eSporting event in world history. Additionally, professional LoL players are now able to get sports visas from the United States government, making LoL a nationally recognised sport. So what is it about these games that make them just as fun to watch as to play?

For starters, much like a real sport, watching an eSport can and will make you better at it. While watching salaried professionals gives players a look at the ultimate possibilities offered by the game, thousands of players streaming online offer varying levels of seriousness with which to watch the game.

YouTube yields tons of 'top plays' and tutorial games by semi-professionals who make money by streaming and offering commentary. Online personalities tied to the game create a shared sense of community among players who all seek to get better or who just like playing. Not only that, but eSports offer the same kind of impossible fame that sports like football and basketball do.

Even though there is a less than 1 per cent chance of getting into the NBA, thousands of kids aspire to just that and work endlessly to improve their game. With a concrete ranking system from bronze at the bottom all the way to the coveted Challenger rank for the top 50 players, eSports like LoL make climbing to the top seem like a distant possibility, but a possibility nonetheless.

Regardless of their popularity, the question remains whether eSports should truly be considered sports at all. For the sake of salaried professional players, it certainly makes sense; after all, to be denied a visa on the grounds that their livelihood is only a game hardly seems fair. These professionals train for months on end perfecting strategies and game mechanics, which led me to consider eSports similar to chess and golf. The mental strain of these games also causes players to get worse with age on a professional level, which I feel supports that argument.

With new strategies coming out every day and patches designed to alter the feel of each game on a regular basis, eSports feel fresh and dynamic in a tournament setting. Certainly performance-enhancing drugs factor in less, which I appreciate. League of Legends even has fantasy leagues online, with amateur LoL players scoring themselves through a roster of professionals based on their performance in a given week. While there may always be naysayers who consider chess, golf and eSports to be detached from 'real' sports like football and basketball, the growing community of eSports players and fans may soon be outnumbering them.

3 December 2013

www.dailycollegian.com

Activities

Brainstorm

1.   What is 'doping'?

2.   What is an eSport?

3.   What is match-fixing?

Oral activities

4.   Are top athletes born or made? Discuss as a group.

5.   'Do eSports qualify as a "real sport"?' Discuss this as a class.

Research activity

6.   Investigate match-fixing. Identify some recent high-profile investigations into suspected fixing. What action do you think should be taken against those found guilty of illegally fixing results? Make some notes that detail your findings and discuss with your class.

Written activities

7.   Watch *Bend it Like Beckham* (12). How does this film explore gender and cultural stereotypes in sport? Write a short essay on your findings.

8.   Read *We don't listen to children when it comes to abuse in sport* (pages 21-22) and write a summary for your local newspaper.

Moral dilemma

9.   Stage a debate where one half of the class argues in favour of performance-enhancing drugs and the other argues against them.

Design activity

10.   Design a poster to highlight the issue of racism in sport.

Key facts

➤ Lesbian and bisexual women are more likely to take part in sport than all women – 44% play sport at least once a week, compared to just over 30% of all women. (page 1)

➤ Sport England's data for 2013/14 shows that 15.6 million adults now play sport at least once a week. That's 1.7 million more than in 2005/6. (page 3)

➤ Currently 40.9% of men play sport at least once a week, compared to 30.3% of women. (page 3)

➤ Age is a factor in participation: 54.5% of 16- to 25-year-olds (58.0% of 14–25-year-olds) take part in at least one sport session a week, compared to 32.0% of older adults (age 26-plus). (page 3)

➤ More disabled people are taking part in sport – latest results show 17.8% are playing sport regularly, up from 15.1% in 2005/6. (page 4)

➤ Over 9.2 million people (16-plus) are members of a sports club – 21% of the English population. (page 4)

➤ Swimming, athletics, cycling, and football are amongst the most popular sports in 2013/14. (page 4)

➤ Nine out of ten primary schools have improved the quality of PE lessons thanks to the £150 million PE and sport premium, new research has shown. (page 9)

➤ Thanks to the PE and sport premium 96% of schools reported improvements in pupils' physical fitness, 93% saw improvements in behaviour and 96% thought the funding had contributed to a healthier lifestyle for their pupils. (page 9)

➤ 46.8 per cent of LGBT students who do not participate in sport find the culture around sport alienating or unwelcoming. (page 12)

➤ A recent study, published by researchers from Edinburgh University and the NSPCC reported widespread emotionally harmful treatment (75%) and unacceptable levels of sexual harassment (29%) in organised sport for children and young people. (page 21)

➤ Nearly four in five football fans (79%) believe there should be a limit on the number of foreign players a Premier League team has in their match-day squad, while about one in six (16%) say there should not be a cap.(page 23)

➤ Reports from fans across Europe consistently show that racism exists in football. Italian football tops the league, with 92% of fans saying it exists in Italian football. England is a close second with 91%, with Spanish fans reporting the lowest incidence of racism, with 73% feeling that it exists. (page 24)

➤ Out of the 380 suspicious European matches identified in the Europol investigation, more than £8 million was generated in betting profits and more than £2 million was paid in bribes. (page 25)

➤ In 2013, the LoL World Championship netted 34 million viewers, making it the biggest eSporting event in world history. (page 26)

Glossary

Athlete – A highly-trained professional or amateur sportsperson.

Doping – The use of performance-enhancing drugs by athletes during sporting competitions. Most of these drugs are illegal and players are required by law to take a drugs test before taking part in competitive events. If it is found that they have taken drugs they will automatically be disqualified from the event, and may also be banned from taking part in any future competitions for a specified period of time.

eSport – Electronic sports (or eSports) refers to competitive gaming events and tournaments (professional gaming). eSports are rapidly gaining popularity and have become a multimillion-dollar industry, featuring major global events attended by thousands and watched by millions. Competitive gaming is claiming a space similar to that of traditional sport and it is a hotly-debated topic as to whether this can be considered a sport or not, and if the players can be called athletes in their own right. This includes video games such as Call of Duty, StarCraft II and League of Legends (LoL).

Hooliganism – A popular term in the past for violence at football matches. Match organisers have worked very hard in recent years to combat hooliganism. Police and other security measures are now routinely put in place to control rioting fans, and repeat 'football hooligans' can be banned from travelling abroad to attend games.

Inclusive sport – Sport which is inclusive does not discriminate on the grounds of gender, ethnicity, sexual orientation or disability. Sport is usually segregated where athletes have a physical difference which makes equal competition difficult – men and women do not generally compete against each other, for example, nor disabled and able-bodied athletes. This is called classification. However, there is no ban on any athlete competing in a separate competition. This is why the term 'sport equity' is sometimes used rather than equality. Athletes should be protected from discrimination and unfair treatment, such as racist and homophobic chanting at football matches.

Match-fixing – Match-fixing is a serious crime and is cheating. This is when someone purposely alters the outcome of a game in exchange for money (a bribe). For example, arranging the use of red and yellow cards or purposely playing poorly in order to throw a game.

Olympic Games – Every four years the Olympic Games are held in a different city around the world. The next summer Olympic Games, which will take place in 2016, are to be held in Rio de Janeiro, Brazil.

Paralympic Games – The Paralympic Games are a series of sporting competitions open to athletes with physical disabilities. They are held immediately following the Olympic Games. Athletes with disabilities including amputations, paralysis and blindness take part in a wide range of competitive sports.